Science in the Renaissance

Brendan January

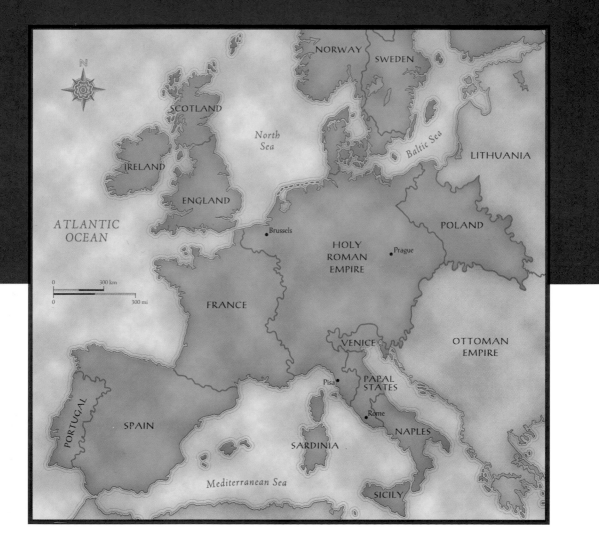

Science in the Renaissance

Brendan January

Science of the Past

FRANKLIN WATTS

A Division of Grolier Publishing
New York • London • Hong Kong • Sydney
Danbury, Connecticut

Visit Franklin Watts on the Internet at: http://publishing.grolier.com

Library of Congress Cataloging-in-Publication Data

January, Brendan, 1972–
    Science in the Renaissance / Brendan January.
        p. cm. — (Science of the past)
    Includes bibliographical references and index.
    Summary: Describes advances in scientific knowledge that occurred during the Renaissance in Europe during the fifteenth and sixteenth centuries.
    ISBN 0-531-11526-7
    1. Science Renaissance—Juvenile literature.   [1. Science—History.   2. Renaissance.] I. Title. II. Series.
Q125.2.J36   1999
509.4'09'031—dc21   97-38633
                                                                         CIP
                                                                         AC

CONTENTS

chapter 1

A New Age

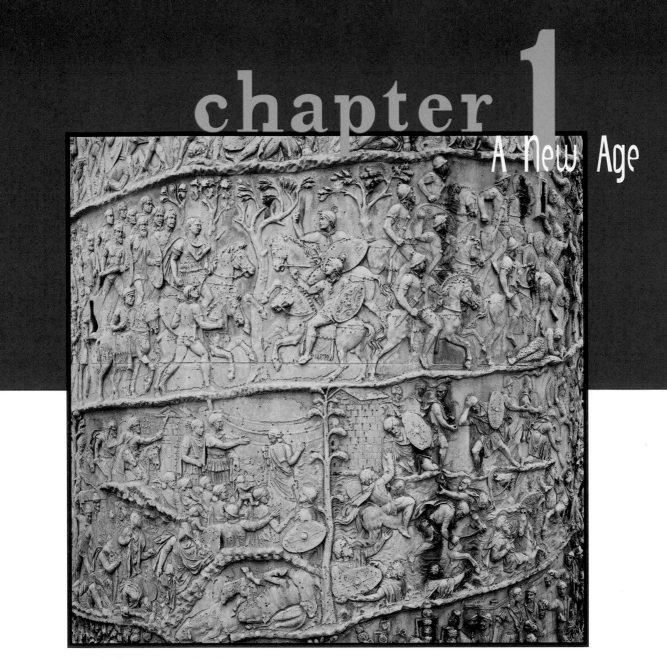

Detail of a column showing Roman
warriors fighting their enemies

During the 1400s and 1500s, a brilliant new age of exploration, creativity, and discovery dawned in Europe. The Europeans called this period the Renaissance, from a Latin word meaning "rebirth." They used this name because the art and science of ancient Greece and Rome was recovered, or reborn, during this age. Inspired by ancient learning, European scientists examined their surroundings with a new attitude. They challenged old beliefs and ideas about God, humankind, and the universe. Their efforts gave birth to modern science.

This detail from a Renaissance painting show two famous Greek philosophers, Plato (left) and Aristotle (right).

Greek and Roman Civilization

More than 1,000 years before the Renaissance, first Greece and then Rome had ruled the ancient world. Greek *philosophers* studied the world around them. They wondered about the workings of nature and theorized about the movements of the stars. Greek sculptors were inspired by the human body.

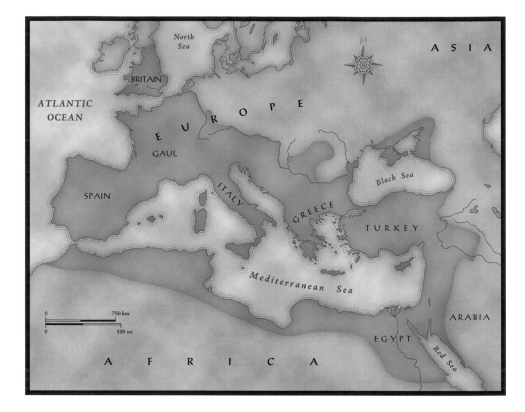

At its height, the Roman Empire included parts of what is now northern Africa, the Middle East, and most of Europe.

In 146 B.C., the Romans conquered Greece and established a huge empire that lasted for centuries. But by the year 350, the Roman Empire began to collapse, and in 476, the last Roman Emperor was overthrown. Eight centuries of art and learning were scattered or destroyed.

After the Roman Empire fell apart, Europe was broken into many small kingdoms and estates. The rulers of these lands spent most of their time fighting with one another. As time passed, the triumphs and achievements of the Greek and Roman *civilizations* were lost or forgotten. Cities were abandoned, bridges collapsed, and paved roads crumbled into dirt trails.

8

The Rise of the Church

In the centuries following the fall of Rome, the Roman Catholic Church rose as the new power in Europe. Christianity spread rapidly, teaching a way of life vastly different from the one valued by Greece and Rome. The Church emphasized the importance of the soul. According to the Church, life on Earth was simply preparation for life in heaven. Church leaders convinced people that all art, literature, and study should be dedicated to the glory of God. The Church discouraged, and sometimes punished, scholars who studied the laws of nature.

As this period—known as the *Medieval Period*—continued, science gradually faded from importance. One Christian leader summed up the attitude of the time: "To discuss the nature of the earth does not help us in our hope of the life to come."

During this period, Greek and Roman culture barely survived. Ancient ruins fell into dust or were buried. Many Greek and Roman texts, however, were saved and

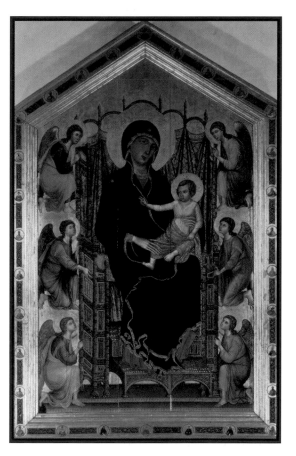

Most Medieval artists painted religious images, such as this representation of *Madonna and Child.*

A monk (above) and three scribes (below) copying ancient texts

copied by Catholic monks living in monasteries. Other texts survived in the Islamic Empire, which dominated areas that are now known as the Middle East and northern Africa. European sailors brought many of these Arabic translations back with them to European cities. In the 1300s, scholars in Europe began to take a great interest in the ancient texts. They discovered incredible writings filled with wisdom and knowledge.

The Renaissance Begins

Through the 1400s and 1500s, the interest in ancient art, science, and literature exploded into the Renaissance. Scholars searched through monastery libraries, seeking ancient Greek and Roman manuscripts. Roman sculpture was discovered and unearthed, its beauty stunning observers. The science and wisdom of the ancient world surged through Europe.

The invention of the printing press in the 1400s allowed Greek and Roman texts to be cheaply reproduced. Suddenly, scholars and students had access to ancient works of literature, philosophy, and science. Influenced by these texts, many scholars became curious about the world around them. One scholar wrote that he was no longer interested in studying heaven and God. Instead, he claimed, "The proper study of man is man!"

This attitude inspired Renaissance scientists to see the world in fresh, exciting ways. Nothing escaped their passionate curiosity and vision. They studied everything from the structure of the human body to the paths of the planets. By the time the Renaissance finally faded in the seventeenth century, modern science had been born.

chapter 2
Drawing the World

A sculptor's studio

One of the most significant discoveries of the Renaissance took place in the studios and workshops of artists—not in a scientist's lab. In fact, most Renaissance artists were also brilliant scientists. Today, most scientists spend their lives studying one subject. Some hack through dense rain forests, searching for new *species* of life. Others observe weather formations and storms. Still others never leave the four walls of their lab. Surrounded by petri dishes and test tubes, they peer through microscopes at worlds teeming with bacteria and viruses.

Renaissance scientists did not limit themselves to just one subject. They were proud of their knowledge of mathematics, art, and *anatomy*. With paintbrushes and pencils, Renaissance scientists observed and recorded the world around them. They noted details. They studied the budding of trees and the way water shatters into thousands of droplets when it cascades over a rock. They

A drawing of a tree done by Leonardo da Vinci

admired the beauty of the human body and were fascinated by the muscles and bones beneath the skin.

One hundred years before the Renaissance, artists were more interested in heaven than Earth. Their art was not intended to reflect the world around them. Renaissance artists and scientists had a different attitude. They were inspired by Greek and Roman art, and they believed that art should mirror the real world. While trying to make their art realistic, Renaissance artists developed a technique called *perspective*.

What Is Perspective?

Perspective is used to give a painting or drawing the appearance of depth. To understand how an artist creates perspective, just imagine yourself standing on a pair of railroad tracks. As you look into the distance, you'll notice that the railroad tracks appear to come closer together. And very far away, the railroad tracks seem to meet! Of course the tracks aren't really any closer together—it's just an illusion.

If you stand on train tracks and look into the distance, you will see that the tracks seem to move closer and closer together.

An artist who wants to make railroad tracks look realistic draws the tracks so that they meet in the center of the picture. This creates the illusion that the tracks are actually going into the distance. When you look at the drawing, you feel like you could ride a train into the picture. The artist has used perspective.

The result is a fantastic appearance of reality. Renaissance artists were thrilled and excited by the possibilities of perspective. They painted and drew buildings, cities, trees, and mountains. No art had ever looked so real.

Do you see how perspective is used in this painting? Hint: Look at the buildings in the background.

Reinassance artists often chose the same subjects as artists who lived during the Medieval Period. Compare the image below to the one on the next page. Each shows the Last Supper—the last meal Jesus Christ ate with his disciples before being crucified.

Using what you have just learned about Reinassance art, try to guess which one was painted by the Medieval artist Duccio di Buoninsegna and which one was painted by Reinassance artist Lucas Cranch, the elder.

Masaccio used
mathematical
calculations to
create the feeling
of depth in his
famous painting
Holy Trinity.

Why is Perspective Important to the Renaissance?

The use of perspective demands a thorough knowledge of a type of mathematics called *geometry*. Geometry includes the study of shapes and angles. The artist Masaccio used precise geometric calculations in his painting *Holy Trinity*. In drawing a cup, artist Paolo Uccello used complex geometric forms to reproduce the cup's structure. Leonardo da Vinci, the brilliant artist and scientist, used perspective to record the passage of a thunderstorm through a valley. The achievements of Renaissance art and its impact on science were enormous. For the first time in history, artists captured the "real world" in their work. They learned how to make detailed observations of nature using the laws of mathematics. And using perspective gave scientists a way to make detailed records of the world as they studied it. As a result, they were able to share their findings with other scholars throughout Europe.

Paolo Ucello's
drawing of a cup

chapter 3
Discovering the Secrets of the Body

Renaissance artist Michelangelo was
inspired by this Greek sculpture.

In 1506, the Italian artist Michelangelo watched as an ancient statue was unearthed in Rome. He never forgot the sight. The statue portrayed a man and his two sons trapped by two giant snakes as they struggled to break free. He was amazed by the way their muscles seemed to ripple and strain in mortal fear.

Inspired by ancient art, Michelangelo and other Renaissance artists devoted countless hours of study to the muscles and tendons that move beneath the body's surface. In order to paint and sculpt the human body perfectly, Michelangelo wanted to *dissect* human bodies. Even though the Church

Michelangelo, who lived from 1475 to 1564, is remembered as one of the greatest artists of all time. His paintings and scuptures of human figures continue to inspire artists today.

frowned on dissection, Michelangelo received help from a local priest who also ran a hospital. The priest allowed Michelangelo to secretly study the bodies in the hospital's morgue.

Leonardo da Vinci: The Art of Anatomy

Leonardo da Vinci shared Michelangelo's desire to understand the workings of the human body. Leonardo also sought every opportunity to perform dissections. One story claims that he sat next to a 100-year-old man and waited for him to die. Leonardo then dissected the body and identified hardening of the arteries as the cause of the man's death.

Leonardo's observations did not stop there. On several occasions, he hauled bodies into his workshop and carefully dissected them by candlelight. The bloody work was unpleasant, and he wrote to a friend that the sight of the dead bodies was often terrifying.

Eventually, Church officials became aware of Leonardo's gruesome practices. In 1514, they charged him with worshiping the dead. Leonardo endured a humiliating trial and was forced to stop his dissections.

By this time, however, Leonardo had made hundreds of anatomical sketches, many of

Leonardo da Vinci was a great artist, inventor, and scientist.

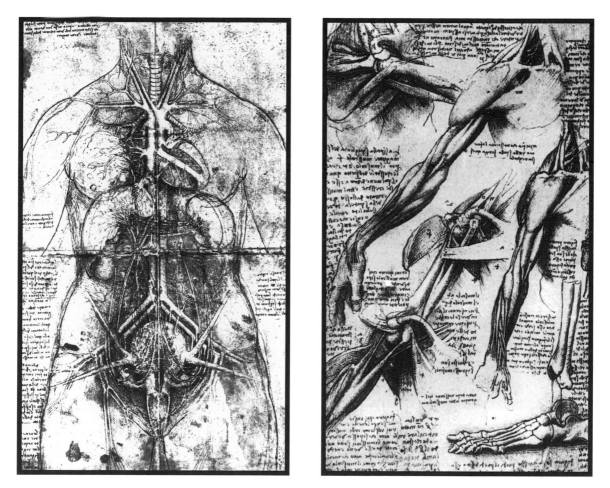

These anatomical drawings, which come from Leonardo daVinci's notebooks, show the heart, lungs, and many of the body's important blood vessels (left) and the muscles of the arm and shoulder (right).

which still survive today. Most of them are both scientifically accurate and beautiful works of art. Leonardo's earliest drawings concentrated on the structure of bones and muscles. He then probed deeper, exploring the inner organs. One of his subjects was a woman who was pregnant when she died. Leonardo sketched the tiny *fetus* inside her womb.

The Notebooks of Leonardo da Vinci

Throughout his life, Leonardo da Vinci recorded his thoughts in a number of notebooks. Nothing escaped his curiosity or passion. His notebooks were filled with sketches of plants, birds, waterfalls, and fantastic machines that would never be built. Leonardo's notebooks are a unique achievement in science and art.

Several mysteries surround the notebooks. No one is certain if Leonardo revealed their contents to other scientists. Some scholars think he discussed his ideas with friends, but others disagree. Consequently, Leonardo's ideas may not have spread beyond the limits of his fantastic imagination.

Leonardo's notebooks are extremely valuable today. Several years ago, one of Leonardo's notebooks was put up for auction and sold to Bill Gates for $30 million.

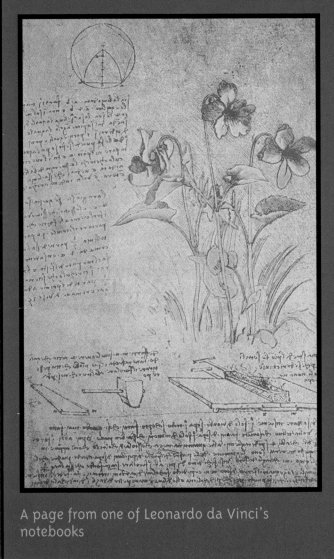

A page from one of Leonardo da Vinci's notebooks

Renaissance Doctors Study the Human Body

While Renaissance artists revealed the mysteries of the human body, Renaissance doctors still clung to old beliefs and ideas. Like the other sciences, Renaissance medicine was dominated by Greek and Roman thinkers who had been dead for more than 1,000 years. The main resource for Renaissance doctors were manuscripts written by a great Roman physician named Galen.

Galen's conclusions on anatomy, however, were misleading and often incorrect. Due to strict Roman laws regarding corpses, Galen could not dissect human bodies. His theories of human anatomy were based on dissections of monkeys, dogs, oxen, and pigs. Galen summarized his observations in a massive book entitled *On the Use of the Parts of the Human Body.*

A Greek healer treating a patient

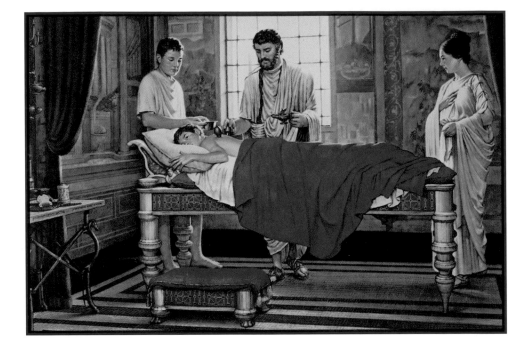

Galen treating a
patient

Through Arabic and Latin translations, the book became the primary medical text throughout Europe.

Early translations of the work were filled with errors and misunderstandings. This frustrated many European physicians who believed Galen to be perfect, and they blamed any mistakes in his work on poor translations. Consequently, many doctors spent more time translating Galen's text than treating diseases and injuries.

Renaissance medical students spent most of their time reading and memorizing Galen. But it soon became obvious that dissecting corpses was the only way to understand how the human body works. Many professors at medical schools hated the idea of cutting open dead bodies. They preferred their books to the bloody mess of the dissecting table. Eventually, however,

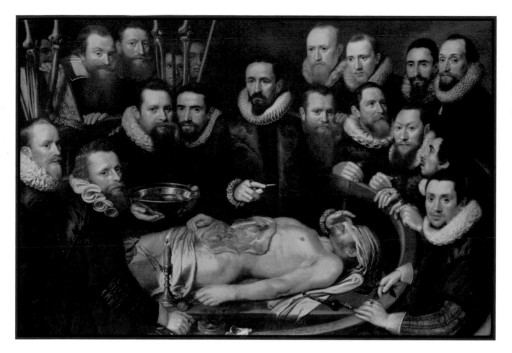

A class of medical students watching their professor dissect a corpse.

dissections were routinely performed in front of large crowds of students.

During these procedures, the professor, often perched in a chair high above the body, read aloud from Galen's book while an assistant dissected the corpse. The bodies were usually those of criminals who had been executed earlier that day. Often, the arrangement of organs within the body contradicted the words being read from Galen's text. When one professor was confronted with this fact, he blamed the body as being abnormal or imperfectly formed.

The dissections themselves were frequently hard to observe. Many of them took place in poorly lit halls. Seated several feet from the table, students strained to see details. Students in the back had little hope of seeing anything at all. One student, Andreas Vesalius, became frustrated with this

Andreas Vesalius revolutionized the study of anatomy. He provided a set of very accurate anatomical diagrams in a book called *The Structures of the Human Body*.

teaching system. He believed that a complete knowledge of the body through dissections should be the basis of every medical education. This belief led Vesalius to change the study of anatomy forever.

The Work of Andreas Vesalius

Vesalius was born in Brussels, Belgium, in 1514. Even as a child, he wanted to understand the mysterious inner structures of the human body. At the age of 23, he became one of the first professors to actually perform dissections himself. Vesalius soon grew dissatisfied with Galen's texts. He noticed several errors in the ancient scientist's work and decided to chart the human body on his own.

For several years, Vesalius took his notes and drawings to artists who carefully made detailed engravings of organs, bones, and muscles. In 1543, Vesalius published these engravings in a book called *The Structures of the Human Body*.

The work was a masterpiece. In the engravings, Vesalius literally peels back the layers of the human body and reveals the structures underneath.

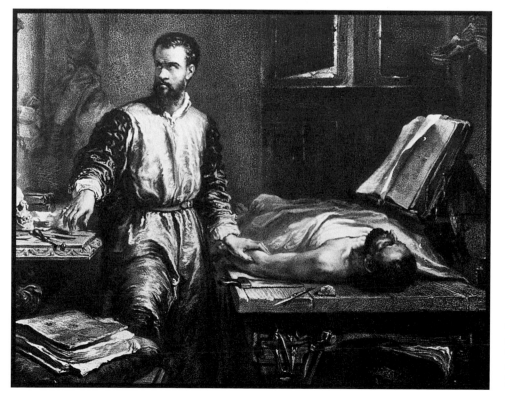

Vesalius spent many hours dissecting and studying the human body.

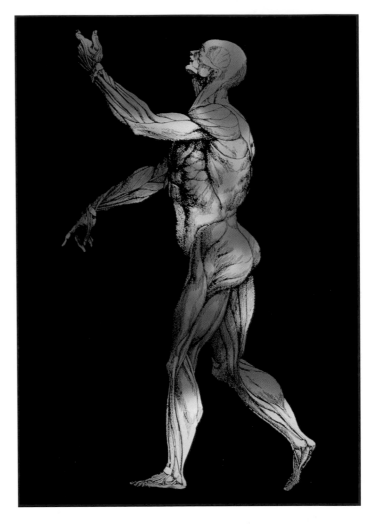

This is a color-enhanced version
of a drawing Vesalius made of the
human muscles.

Complex muscle patterns and bone formations are clearly explained and
labeled. For the first time in history, the human body had been accurately
mapped and illustrated. The printing press soon made Vesalius's work
available throughout Europe. While Vesalius challenged Galen in anatomy, another doctor questioned ancient ideas about the causes of and
treatments for diseases.

Paracelus rejected the Greek idea that sickness was caused by an imbalance in the body. He believed that each disease had a specific cause and should be treated in a specific way.

Paracelsus Takes a Fresh Look at Disease

Paracelsus was born in Switzerland in 1493. As a young boy, he learned basic medicine and chemistry from his father. When Paracelsus was 14 years old, he began attending classes at several universities. He had hoped to become a doctor, but the universities and their professors disappointed him. He wrote, "The universities do not teach all things, so a doctor must seek out old wives, gypsies, sorcerers, wandering tribes, old robbers, and such outlaws and take lessons from them."

Ancient doctors had believed that the body consisted of four elements— earth, air, water, and fire. In a healthy body, these elements were thought

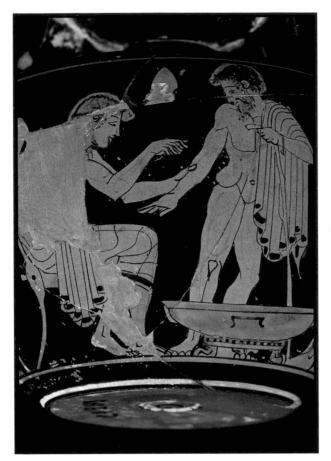

Bleeding a patient, or bloodletting, was a common treatment in ancient Greece.

to be in perfect balance. In an unhealthy body, one of the elements outweighed the other three. For example, the body grew feverish from an excess of fire. Too much water caused chills. To combat disease, doctors tried to restore the balance of elements in the body. One treatment was *bloodletting*, a method that killed more patients than it cured. Other doctors insisted that disease was God's punishment for sin. They believed in curing the soul to restore health to the body.

Paracelsus rejected these ideas. In front of cheering students, Paracelsus tossed books written by ancient doctors into a raging bonfire. Paracelsus stressed the healing power of nature.

Paracelsus's opinion of ancient medicine took shape while he was still quite young. He grew up in a mining town where many workers became sick with a disease called miners' sickness. Several local doctors believed the miners had fallen victim to the spirits in the mountains. Paracelsus thought this was ridiculous. He believed that the disease was caused by metallic fumes.

Later, Paracelsus studied a sexually transmitted disease called syphilis. After careful examinations, he suggested a treatment of limited amounts of mercury. For the first time, a doctor had identified a disease as a separate illness with specific symptoms. Paracelsus claimed that each disease had to be observed and then treated separately. Illness was not the result of an imbalance within the body. For each disease, there was a cure. Paracelsus's ideas launched modern medicine.

While Paracelsus and Vesalius revealed the mysteries of the human body, other Renaissance scientists turned their attention to the sky. For thousands of years, people had gazed at the stars and planets, wondering and guessing at the plan behind it all. In the Renaissance, this baffling mystery was at last solved.

chapter 4
Revealing the Mysteries of the Universe

Renaissance astronomers challenged
Greek ideas about the stars and
planets.

To the ancient Greeks, the stars were part of a beautiful and distant world. The Greek philosopher Aristotle believed that the material found in stars was completely different from the substances that make up our own planet. On Earth, mountains erode, rivers dry up or flood, and the seasons come and go. Far above the rapidly changing Earth, however, the stars glow peacefully night after night.

To the dismay of ancient *astronomers*, however, some stars did not act like the others. Instead of simply moving across the night sky, these stars sped up and slowed down, some-

An alabaster bust of the Greek philosopher Aristotle

times they even backed up! These movements baffled early Greek astronomers. Why didn't these stars move predictably? The Greeks called them "planets," meaning "wandering ones."

A painting of
Claudius Ptolemaeus
done by an Italian
artist around 1475

Ptolemy Explains the Universe

In the second century, the ancient astronomer Claudius Ptolemaeus, better know as Ptolemy, proposed a theory that solved the puzzle of the planets. Ptolemy observed the nightly journey of the stars as they rose in the east, passed overhead, and set in the west. The sun made the same journey during the day. Ptolemy theorized that the sun, planets, and stars orbited Earth, while the Earth sat, unmoving, at the center of the universe.

Ptolemy wrote his theory in a massive work, *Mathematical Composition.* Later, Arab scholars were so impressed with the theory that they renamed the work *Almagest,* which means "the greatest."

An artist's interpretation of a model of the universe proposed by Ptolemy

Ptolemy's theory was accepted as the first true model of the universe. But as time passed, observers noticed that Ptolemy's charts were far from accurate. Planets often appeared in the wrong place at the wrong time. When Ptolemy's theory failed, scholars modified it.

By the time of the Renaissance, Ptolemy's model had grown hopelessly complicated and ugly. Greek philosophers had insisted that the universe was a simple, beautiful creation. Ptolemy's model for the universe, however, was filled with corrections and cycles, all trying to explain the movements of the stars and planets. Finally, in the Renaissance, new theories replaced Ptolemy's ancient model.

Copernicus Rejects Ptolemy's Model

Nicolaus Copernicus was born in 1473 in Poland. He spent his young adult years studying mathematics, astronomy, law, and medicine at the University of Kraków. Copernicus loved ancient Greek and Roman literature. He poured over the dialogues of the Greek philosopher Plato and studied the philosophy of Aristotle. His private library included two copies of Ptolemy's *Almagest.*

Plato's philosophy assumed that the universe had a simple design. Inspired by Plato, Copernicus rejected the *Ptolemaic system.* He began to search for other possible models of the universe. While reading an obscure work, Copernicus made a startling discovery. Some ancient Greek philosophers had suggested that the sun, not Earth, was the center of the universe. Copernicus was further encouraged by a school of philosophy called *Neoplatonism*, which emphasized the importance of the sun. Copernicus began to speculate that the sun was in fact at the center of the universe.

This was a dangerous idea. According to the Bible and the Roman Catholic Church, Earth was the center of the universe. Anyone disputing this belief risked the anger of Church officials. The 1500s were rocked with violent religious battles, and the Church did not tolerate protests against its teachings. Those who did not agree with the Church could be tried as *heretics* in a religious court. If the court ruled that Copernicus's theory was heresy, he could be condemned to death.

Copernicus decided to be cautious. Quietly, he sent his theory

Nicholaus Copernicus proposed that the sun is at the center of the solar system and that all the planets revolve around it.

to thinkers and scientists throughout Europe. The idea spread quickly, inspiring some and angering others. "Earth moves?" the skeptics demanded. The concept seemed to insult common knowledge! "If Earth moves, wouldn't buildings fall down?" they asked.

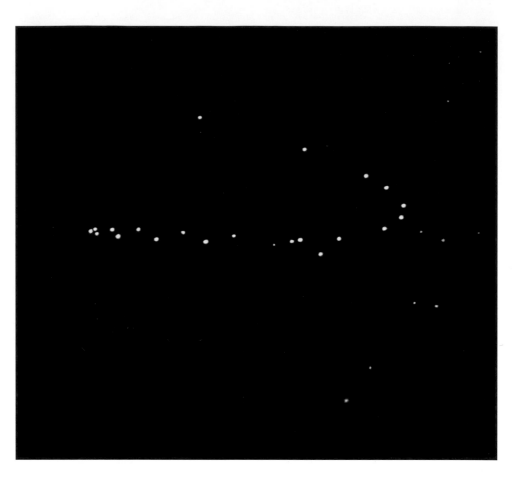

Copernicus answered his critics with an example. To the crew on a moving ship, it seems that the ship is standing still, and that the shore is moving past them. People on Earth are like the sailors on a ship. Although Earth is actually moving, it appears that the sun and the stars are moving past us.

Copernicus's theory also addressed one of the most nagging puzzles in *astronomy*—the movement of the planet Mars. As Mars moves through the night sky, it occasionally appears to stop, back up, and then move forward again. This event had fascinated and frustrated scholars for centuries.

According to Copernicus's model, Earth is closer to the sun than Mars. This means that Earth's *orbit* is inside Mars's orbit. As Earth moves around the sun, it sometimes passes by Mars. To observers on Earth, it appears that Mars stops and backs up. Each orbit, the cycle repeats itself.

Copernicus finally approved publication of his new theories in a book called *On the Revolutions of the Heavenly Spheres*. The first published edition reached him on May 23, 1543—the day before he died.

Copernicus was wise to wait. As soon as his book was published, religious leaders declared him a heretic. Martin Luther, a famous religious leader, thundered, "This fool wishes to reverse the entire science of astronomy! But sacred scripture tells us that Joshua commanded the sun to stand still, and not the earth." Copernicus's masterpiece was condemned by the pope and placed on the Church's list of forbidden books.

Why all this controversy? Copernicus's theory did more than just challenge the Church, it disputed the way Medieval society viewed the world and the universe. According to Medieval philosophy, Earth was completely different and separate from the stars and planets. On Earth, things change, but the stars do not. They stay the same forever, like God Himself. Copernicus's theory threatened to destroy this way of thinking. According to Copernicus, Earth moves around the sun like any other planet. He believed the entire universe obeys the same laws of motion. There is no separation between heaven and Earth.

Copernicus's theory, however, had major flaws. While he correctly theorized that the planets orbit the sun, he also insisted that planets orbit in perfect circles. (Today, we know that planets orbit in elongated circles, or ovals, called *ellipses*.) Copernicus worked diligently to gather evidence that would prove his theory correct, but the planets repeatedly appeared in locations that defied his calculations. When Copernicus died in 1543, the night skies were still a mystery.

For the next century, Copernicus's theory remained the subject of angry debate. Anyone caught teaching or supporting his ideas risked imprisonment or death. Despite this, his book became popular among many astronomers and intellectuals. Support for Ptolemy's theory was fading in the face of new evidence.

An artist's interpretation of a model of the universe proposed by Copernicus

According to Aristotle and Ptolemy, change in the heavens was impossible. But in 1574, a *supernova* suddenly appeared as a bright smudge in the night sky. Caused by the massive explosion of a very large star, supernovae can burn for several years. One astronomer was so shocked at the appearance of the "new star," that he wrote: "I began to doubt the faith of my own eyes."

Tycho Brahe Studies the Stars

The man who made that observation was the Danish astronomer Tycho Brahe. Like Copernicus, Brahe was drawn to astronomy at an early age.

Although his parents insisted he study law, Brahe was fascinated with the night sky. He secretly purchased several books on astronomy and began to study them. A careful and painstaking young man, Brahe soon grew disgusted with the inaccuracies of Ptolemy's models. He resolved to map the universe with far more accuracy than any astronomer had dreamed possible.

The money to fund his project came from a tragedy. Brahe's foster father had saved Frederick II, king of Denmark and Norway, from drowning in a river, but caught pneumonia and died soon after. Frederick II, grateful for his life, decided to fund Brahe's research. Brahe used the money to construct an elaborate observatory on the island of Ven, which sits between Denmark and Sweden. Night after night, Brahe studied the sky, taking careful measurements of the stars and planets. Brahe and his assistants carved their observations into a brass ball 5 feet (1.5 m) in diameter. As he recorded the movements of the planets, Brahe attempted to create a new model of the universe. Brahe's skill, however, was in observation. None of his theories were any improvement over those proposed by Ptolemy.

Tycho Brahe made careful measurements of the positions of the stars and planets.

An artist's representation of Brahe's observatory

Johannes Kepler Settles the Dispute

On February 4, 1600, Johannes Kepler arrived to work with Brahe in a new observatory in Prague, Czechoslovakia. As a young student, Kepler was firmly committed to the *Copernican system*. Kepler believed that God had laid out the universe according to mathematical laws. He hoped to use Brahe's new astronomical data to discover these laws and revise Copernicus's theory into a usable model.

Brahe, however, sensed Kepler's brilliance and grew jealous. He concealed most of his data from Kepler, revealing only small bits of information at meals. When Kepler became furious and threatened to leave, Brahe gave Kepler the right to observe and chart one planet—Mars. Kepler wrote: "When he saw that I had a darling mind, he thought the best way to deal with me would be to give me my head, to let me choose the observations of one single planet, Mars."

Copernicus had explained the basic movements of Mars, but no one had been able to calculate its orbit mathematically. Brahe was far from generous when he allowed Kepler to observe Mars. Of all the planets, Mars

Johannes Kepler used Brahe's data and his own observations to disprove Copernicus's model of the universe.

45

An image of Mars based on data collected by the Viking *Orbiter*

was the most mystifying. But Kepler was confident. He boasted that he would be able to explain the planet's confusing orbit in 8 days.

Eight years after his boast, Kepler was still trying solve the puzzle. He called it "my war on Mars." Kepler tried to imagine how Earth's orbit would look from Mars. After hundreds of pages of calculations, the answer still eluded him. The problem was that Kepler kept trying to fit the orbit of Mars into a perfect circle. Eventually, however, he stumbled on an astonishing and radical idea—the planets' orbits were not perfect circles at all; they were ellipses.

Finally, Kepler had found the solution. He calculated the orbits of all the planets and concluded that each planet orbited in an ellipse. This discovery is known today as Kepler's first law of planetary motion. In the next 10 years, Kepler formulated two more laws that accurately predicted the movements of planets.

Kepler's laws solved problems that had occupied the greatest minds for thousands of years. In 1609, Kepler published his discoveries in his book *Astronomica Nova*. The Copernican revolution was practically complete, and the plan of the universe was at last in his grasp. "I contemplate its beauty with incredible and ravishing delight," wrote Kepler.

European scientists and religious scholars remained divided over Kepler's conclusions. Resistance to the Copernican system was still strong, particularly from religious authorities. Although Kepler had practically proved that planets move, he did not understand the force that caused the movement. *Gravity,* the attraction of one mass to another, remained a mystery.

chapter 5
Galileo Galilei: Pioneer of Physics

Galileo Galilei was a great physicist
and astronomer.

On February 14, 1564, Galileo Galilei was born in the Italian city of Pisa. As a young man, Galileo studied to become a doctor. He soon grew restless, however, and he dropped out. In 1583, Galileo began studying mathematics with a family friend. The subject fascinated him. Within 10 years, he became a professor of mathematics at the University of Pisa. Galileo believed that a knowledge of mathematics was essential to understanding the world and the universe. "The Book of Nature," he said, "is written in mathematics."

At that time, the theories of the ancient Greek philosopher Aristotle dominated mathematics and physics. Aristotle believed that the earth and sky were made from four elements—earth, air, fire, and water—and that each element moved to its natural place in the universe.

For example, Greek scientists noticed that fire burns upward, so they concluded that fire naturally belongs above the air in the sky. They also observed that water rolls down hillsides and returns to the sea. The Greeks concluded that the water returns to the place where it naturally belongs. When Greeks watched objects fall to the ground, they reasoned that their rightful place is at the center of the universe.

Aristotle also theorized that heavy objects fall faster than light ones. This seemed so obvious that few people had actually tested this idea with an experiment.

Galileo grew dissatisfied with Aristotle's ideas. According to one story, Galileo spent an afternoon watching a hailstorm. He noticed that both

This terra-cotta figure of Galileo is on display at the Science Museum in London, England.

large hailstones and small hailstones hit the ground at the same time. This contradicted Aristotle's theory that heavier objects fall faster than lighter ones. Inspired by his observation, Galileo performed an experiment. He constructed a small ramp and measured the amount of time it took for various weights to reach the bottom. As he had anticipated, they all moved at about the same speed.

Another legend says that Galileo climbed the famous Leaning Tower of Pisa and leaned over the top. Before a crowd of observers, Galileo released a large cannonball and a small musket ball. According to Aristotle, the cannonball should fall faster than the musketball. It did not. The two objects struck the ground at the same time. Faced with this evidence, Galileo theorized that objects fall at the same speed regardless of their weight. Elements do not move because it is "natural fulfillment," but because a force acts upon them. Galileo had refuted 1,500 years of Aristotelian philosophy.

Galileo's radical ideas made him few friends. The University of Pisa did not renew his teaching contract, and he was forced to find another teaching post at the University of Padua. Despite these troubles, Galileo published his new ideas and they circulated throughout Europe.

Galileo and the Telescope

In 1609, Galileo learned of a new device being constructed in Holland—the telescope. At that time, people used telescopes to spot ships or watch hostile armies. It occurred to Galileo, however, that the telescope could be useful for observing the night sky. He quickly grasped the principles of the new invention and constructed his own telescope.

Galileo was shocked when he viewed the moon. Instead of having a

Galileo challenged Aristotle's ideas about how and why objects fall to Earth. This sketch is a representation of a legend about the experiment Galileo did to show that an object's weight does not affect how fast it falls.

An image of Jupiter and the four moons first viewed by Galileo in 1610.

smooth, glassy surface, the moon was pockmarked with craters. Galileo wrote with astonishment that the moon is "rough and uneven, covered everywhere—just like the earth—with huge mountains, valleys, and chasms."

More discoveries followed. Galileo counted four moons orbiting the planet Jupiter. Galileo believed this observation proved that Copernicus was correct. Just as the moons orbit Jupiter, so do the planets orbit the sun.

Next, Galileo pointed his telescope toward the Milky Way. To his surprise, what appeared to be a huge band of light was actually billions of individual stars. The stars also seemed to be spread out and scattered. Until then, philosophers and scientists had assumed that all stars were the same distance from Earth. Galileo's observations suggested that some stars are closer to Earth than others.

In 1610, Galileo published his observations in a book that he called *Starry Messenger.* With great daring, Galileo supported Copernicus's theory that Earth revolves around the sun.

The book caused a sensation in Europe, and critics immediately attacked Galileo. In 1616, the pope called Galileo to Rome and demanded that he reject Copernicus's theories. Fearing that he would be branded a heretic, Galileo agreed. He returned to Florence and spent the next few years quietly studying less controversial subjects.

In 1632, however, Galileo published *Dialogue Concerning the Two Chief World Systems.* The book disputed the ancient belief that Earth and the heavens were separate. Galileo proposed that the planets, the stars, and Earth were made of the same substances. Galileo also theorized that the laws of motion observed on Earth affect the movements of objects in the heavens. Galileo's book undermined assumptions that had ruled science for more than 1,000 years, and it also opened Galileo to charges of heresy.

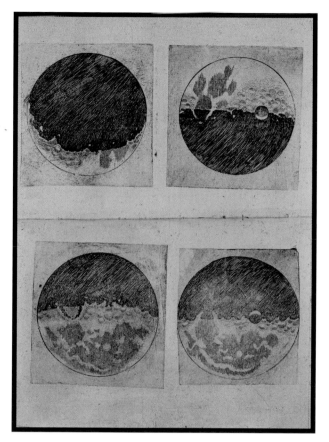

Galileo made these sketches of the moon and included them in his book *Starry Messenger.*

Galileo and the Inquisition

Five months after *Dialogue* was published, Galileo was ordered to appear before a religious court, called the *Inquisition*, in Rome. The charges were very serious. If Galileo was found guilty, he could be put to death. Like Copernicus's theory, Galileo's book threatened to discredit the Christian view of the world. Church officials believed that God created Earth for humankind and the heavens for Himself. The planets were kept in orbit by angels, who pushed them in eternal circles. Suggesting that there was no separation between heaven and Earth was like saying that there was no heaven—or God—at all.

Galileo arrived in Rome confident that he could simply reason with the court. But he soon realized that the court had no intention of hearing his argument. On April 30, 1633, Galileo admitted he had been full of pride and false reasoning. Kneeling before the court, he said that Earth did not move, and that his book had been wrong. He signed a confession that stated his firm rejection of the Copernican system. The Church banned his book, and Galileo spent the rest of his life under house arrest. On January 8, 1642, Galileo died and was buried in a small church.

Although the Church had silenced Galileo, it could not stop the truth in his ideas. Across Europe, scientists and scholars began making their own observations with telescopes. They soon discovered that Galileo's conclusions were frequently accurate. By crushing Galileo, the Church undermined its own authority. Galileo became a symbol of resistance against an arrogant and dangerous power, and his books were eagerly read throughout Europe.

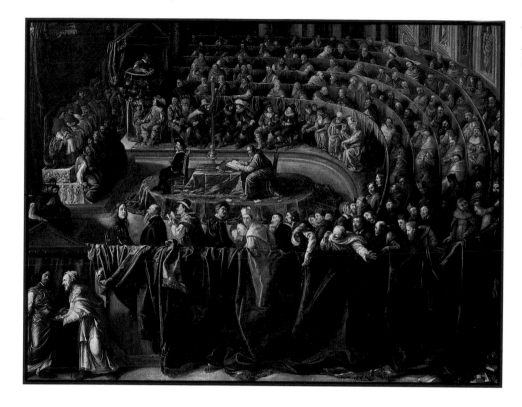

Galileo at his trial before the Inquisition

Galileo rejected the idea that philosophy or religion could explain the universe. Instead, he declared that nature worked according to mathematical rules. The scientist must use experiments to understand these rules. Galileo used mathematics and observation to study light, sound, and heat. Many methods used by modern scientists can be found in Galileo's writings.

Galileo's breakthrough was the final result of a long and extensive process. It began with the Renaissance artists, who observed and drew the world around them. Galileo insisted that the scientist, like the artist, must observe nature and record it exactly. From observations and experiments, scientists can determine the mathematical laws that rule the natural world. This process survives today as the *scientific method.*

chapter6
The Impact of Renaissance Science

Although we have understood Earth's place in the solar system since the Renaissance, we did not have a sense of what our planet really looks like until this image was taken by the crew of Apollo 17 in 1972.

By the time the Renaissance drew to a close in the seventeenth century, people's view of the world and the universe had been changed forever. A few brilliant scientists, Copernicus, Brahe, and Kepler, caused this change.

Their observations proved that Earth was a planet like any other. It revolves around the sun. The heavens are not separate—above and apart—from Earth.

The human body no longer kept its secrets. Through Vesalius's patient diagramming, its muscles, blood vessels, and organs had been precisely mapped. Paracelsus discredited the idea that disease was an imbalance within the body, or God's punishment for our sins. He taught that each disease has symptoms that must be observed and identified before the patient is treated. The groundwork for modern medicine was laid.

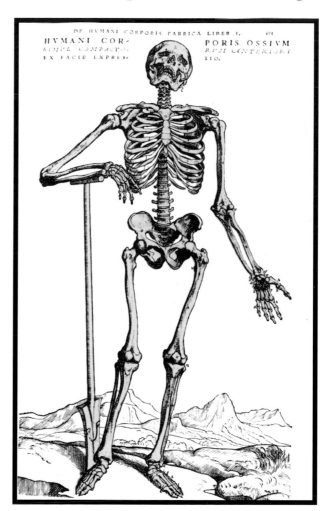

A diagram of the human skeleton from Vesalius's book

The life and work of Galileo summarized many of the achievements and characteristics of Renaissance science. His trial before the Inquisition made him famous. Throughout Europe, his ideas gathered strength while the power of the Church faded. Most importantly, his ideas of experimentation and emphasis on mathematics gained wide acceptance among scientists. Galileo's conceptions became an important part of the modern scientific method.

The Renaissance affected every branch of science, but it also changed science itself. Scientists began looking at the world differently. They used new methods and tools to perform experiments and examine data. This is the genuine triumph of the Renaissance—science became a force equal to religion and philosophy. Today, we understand much about our world because of the spirit of science launched in the Renaissance.

GLOSSARY

anatomy —the study of the body's structure.

astronomer—a scientist who studies stars and planets.

astronomy—the scientific study of the stars and planets.

bloodletting—drawing blood from the body. In the past, some healers believed that removing some blood from the body could cure some diseases.

civilization—a community of people with a relatively high level of cultural development.

Copernican system—the belief that the planets orbit around the sun.

dissect—to cut up a body to study the structure inside.

ellipse—an oval drawn around two points.

fetus—an unborn human in the very early stages of development.

geometry—a branch of mathematics that deals with the measurement of areas and the relationships between shapes and angles.

gravity—the force of attraction between objects.

heretic—someone who disputes the accepted teachings of the Roman Catholic Church.

Inquisition—a Roman Catholic court that tried cases of heresy during the sixteenth and seventeenth centuries.

Medieval Period—the years between the fall of Rome and the Renaissance. It was characterized by the rise of the Roman Catholic Church and the decline of science.

Neoplatonism—a school of thought based on the philosophy of Plato.

orbit—the path of a planet as it rotates around the sun.

perspective—a technique that gives depth to a drawing or painting.

philosopher—a person who studies reality and the nature of truth.

Ptolemaic system—the system of thought that placed Earth in the center of the universe. It is named after Ptolemy, a Greek mathematician and astronomer who lived in Alexandria, Egypt, around the year 100.

scientific method—a system of investigation.

species—a group of organisms within a genus that share certain common characteristics. Members of a species can mate and produce young.

supernova—the explosion of a massive star.

RESOURCES

Books

Beshore, George. *Science in Early Islamic Culture*. Danbury, CT: Franklin Watts, 1998.

Ganeri, Anita. *How Would You Survive as an Ancient Roman?* London: Watts, 1995.

Gay, Kathlyn. *Science in Ancient Greece*. Danbury, CT: Franklin Watts, 1998.

Harris, Jacquelin L. *Science in Ancient Rome*. Danbury, CT: Franklin Watts, 1998.

Kerr, Daisy. *Ancient Greeks*. Danbury, CT: Franklin Watts, 1996.

Nardo, Don. *Life in Ancient Greece*. San Diego: Lucent Books, 1996.

Ronan, Colin A. *Science: Its History and Development*. New York: Facts on File, 1982.

Simon, Charnan. *Explorers of the Ancient World*. Chicago: Children's Press, 1990.

Starr, Chester G. *A History of the Ancient World*. London: Oxford, 1983.

Internet Sites

The Art of Renaissance Science gives a general overview of scientific discoveries made during the Renaissance. Special attention is given to the work of Galileo and the use of perspective in drawings and paintings. It can be reached at **http://bang.lanl.gov/video/stv/arshtml/arstoc.html.**

Beginner's Guide to Research in the History of Science has a section devoted to scientific developments of the Renaissance. It also has links to primary resource material The address for this site is **http://www.kaiwan.com/~lucknow/horus/guide/tp1.html.**

Exploring Ancient World Culture includes maps, timelines, essays, and images that describe ancient civilizations in Rome and Greece as well as China, and the Near East. It can be reached at **http://eawc.evansville.edu/index.htm.**

The Galileo Project is an excellent resource for information related to the life and work of Galileo. It includes maps and a timeline. Its address is **http://es.rice.edu/ES/humsoc/Galileo/.**

ABOUT THE AUTHOR

Brendan January was born and raised in Pleasantville, New York. He attended Haverford College, where he received a B.A. in History and English. He has written a number of children's books about American history. This is his first book for Franklin Watts.